Animal World
MAMMALS

Edited by: Pallabi B. Tomar, Hitesh Iplani

Managing editor: Tapasi De

Designed by: Vijesh Chahal, Anil Kumar & Rohit Kumar

Illustrated by: Suman S. Roy, Tanoy Choudhury

Colouring done by: Vinay Kumar, Kiran Kumari & Pradeep Kumar

CONTENTS

What are mammals?

Mammals are vertebrates that evolved in the Jurassic Period, about 175 million years ago. They range in size from the minute Bumblebee Bat which measures a mere 4 cm to the colossal Blue Whale which can reach lengths of 100 ft and is the largest animal on this planet. Common mammals include rodents, bats, dogs, bears, cats, deer, sheep, goats, and humans. In all, there are about 5,400 species of mammals, distributed in about 1,200 genera, 153 families, and 29 orders.

The animals which give birth to their young ones and suckle them are known as mammals. Mammals have mammary glands to feed their young ones with milk from these glands. They have lungs to respire. Mammals are warm blooded animals and have hairs on their body. The animals that come under this category have many differences. For example, bat, seal and the cow, however come under this category but they have nothing common. Man also comes under the category of mammals. Mammals live in different places as some live on trees, on land, in water and inside the earth. Some of the mammals are carnivorous they eat only flesh; whereas others are herbivorous they eat only grass. Some mammals are both carnivorous and herbivorous they eat both flesh and grass.

Astonishing fact

Bats are the only mammals that can fly.

The evolution of mammals

Mammals are believed to have evolved from an ancient group of reptiles called the therapsids. Therapsids lived about 225 million years ago during the Triassic Period. As they evolved, therapsids developed a lighter, more flexible skeleton and the alignment of their limbs changed over time to be directly beneath their body.

The first mammals are thought to have been somewhat small creatures (less than 10 cm long) with light, delicate skeletons. The fossil record suggests that these creatures had teeth and skulls characteristic of herbivores or predators that fed on arthropods or other vertebrates. Well-developed senses of hearing and smell suggest they may have been nocturnal creatures. Another important adaptation mammals displayed was the ability to regulate their own body temperatures.

When climate change took place in the Mesozoic Era, temperatures fluctuated and dropped. The reptiles that once dominated the land suffered in the low temperatures, while mammals were able to better compete since their body temperatures were less affected by temperature variation.

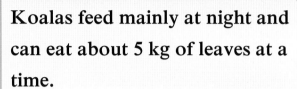

Astonishing fact

Koalas feed mainly at night and can eat about 5 kg of leaves at a time.

The Tertiary period, which began about 70 million years ago, brought with it the dawning of the 'age of mammals', a time following the extinction of many reptile species. This is when mammals diversified significantly in number and kind.

Before long, different groups of mammals had become adapted to a great variety of ecological niches, many previously occupied by dinosaurs. The key to mammalian success in their wide variety of lifestyles was an amazing structural and functional plasticity. Limbs were variously modified into flippers, shovels, wings, and pillars. Teeth became adapted to dealing efficiently with diets ranging from a myriad of plant material through a variety of animal material, including insects and marine invertebrates as well as other mammals.

Types of mammals

There are three main types of mammals: monotremes, marsupials, and placental mammals.

Monotremes: The monotremes are primitive egg-laying mammals. Modern-day monotremes include the echidnas (spiny ant-eaters) and the duck-billed platypus.

Monotremes are the most primitive and there are only three species: the duck-billed platypus and two species of echidna. These mammals have hair and produce milk, but they also lay eggs. The eggs are leathery, similar to reptile eggs, and hatch into tiny young that are not well developed. The young cling to the fur on the mother's belly and suck at her milk, which comes from pores in the skin instead of from a nipple.

Duck-billed platypus

Marsupials: Marsupials are another group of mammals. They have tiny, undeveloped young, but they grow inside the mother's body instead of in an egg. When they are born, they climb up the mother's fur to a pouch on her belly and settle inside. Some well-known marsupials are koalas and kangaroos.

Placental mammals: Placental mammals are the largest group, and their young develop inside the mother's body while attached to a placenta. This is an organ that gives them nutrients and oxygen from the mother's blood and it allows them to

Koala

grow and develop to a more advanced stage before being born. Some examples of placental mammals are cats, bears, monkeys, and humans.

Astonishing fact

There are more than 350 breeds of ponies and horses.

Characteristics of mammals

Mammals display a remarkable range of adaptations that enable them to inhabit a wide range of habitats. Some of their characteristics are shared by no other groups of animals: hair, mammary glands, and three specialized middle-ear bones.

The first characteristic that guarantees that an animal is a mammal is that it (if it is female) can produce milk to feed its young. This milk is produced by modified sweat glands called 'mammary' glands. It is from these glands that the whole group takes its name 'Mammals.'

Hair is a defining characteristic of mammals. No other organisms possess true hair and all mammals have hair covering at least part of their body at some time during their life. An individual hair consists of a rod of cells that are reinforced by a protein known as keratin. Hair grows from skin cells called follicles. Hair can take on several different forms including fur, whiskers, spines, or horns. Hair serves numerous functions. It can provide insulation, protect the skin, serve as camouflage, and provide sensory feedback.

The lower jaw in mammals is a single bone on either side. In all other vertebrates there is more than one bone on each side of the jaw.

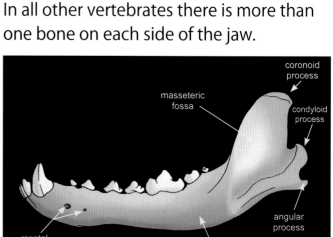

coronoid process
masseteric fossa
condyloid process
mental foramen
mandi bular body
angular process

Astonishing fact

Vampire bats feed entirely on blood which is freshly drawn from small wounds inflicted on prey such as cattle, horses, pig, etc.

There are three bones in the middle ear of every mammal. They are the malleus, incus, and stapes which are more commonly known as the hammer, anvil and stirrups respectively. These bones help mammals in hearing by transferring sound waves from the eardrum to the inner ear.

Mammals have a unique heart. Although mammals have a four chambered heart like birds, the main artery turns left, as it leaves the heart. In birds it turns to the right, whereas, in all other vertebrates, there are more than one artery that originate from the heart.

Finally mammals have a diaphragm. It is a sheet of muscle and tendon that separates the body cavity into two sections. Heart and lungs are before/ above, and the liver, kidneys, stomach, intestines, etc, are behind/below. No other animal has a diaphragm.

mammal ear

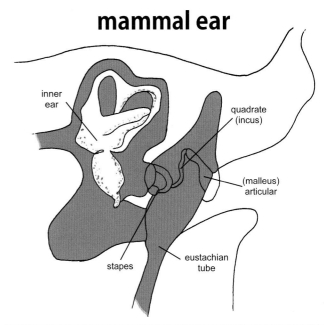

inner ear

quadrate (incus)

(malleus) articular

stapes

eustachian tube

Astonishing fact

The Giant anteater eats over 10,000,000 ants or termites a year.

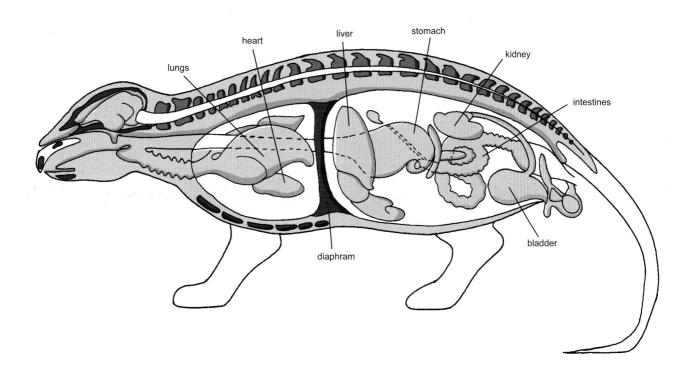

lungs

heart

liver

stomach

kidney

intestines

diaphram

bladder

Where do mammals live?

Underground mammals

Some small mammals spend all or most of their lives living underground. These include many species of prairie dogs, chipmunks, moles, groundhogs, Greenland collared lemmings, and Peruvian tuco-tucos. Each of these mammals has a special body design enabling it to survive underground.

Groundhog

Sea mammals

Some mammals live in the sea, including manatees, whales, seals, and dolphins.

Whale

Astonishing fact

The world's largest rodent is the Capybara.

While some need air every few minutes, a sperm whale can remain underwater for an hour and a half. Some sea mammals have a very low metabolism. They don't use up their oxygen quickly and can store large amounts of oxygen in their bodies.

Eastern pygmy possum

Tree mammals

Some mammals spend all or most of their lives in trees. Tree-dwelling mammals are often hidden from sight by leaves, vines, and branches. Tree-dwelling mammals include the Eastern pygmy possum, which nests in small tree hollows; the koala, Lumholtz's tree kangaroo, which leaps from branch to branch; the three-toed sloth and the clouded leopard.

Flying mammals

The only truly flying mammals are bats. The sound of bat wings was first heard about 50 million years ago. Some bats are large, with a wingspan almost 7 ft (21.3 m) wide. Some are small, as the Philippine bamboo bat, whose body is just 2 inches (5.08 cm) long.

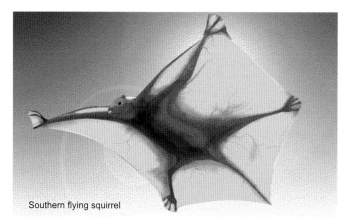
Southern flying squirrel

Other mammals only appear to fly, such as the Southern flying squirrel and the colugo or Malayan flying lemur. These mammals have gliding membranes, skin folds from body front to legs, that, when spread out, act almost like a parachute.

Desert mammals

Some mammals spend most of their lives in very dry areas. Desert dwelling mammals include the North African elephant shrew, white-tailed antelope squirrel, and the desert kangaroo rat. No mammal can live without water. Desert rodents have a way of getting water from their own body functions. Rodents may also get water by eating plants, seeds, roots, and insects that contain water.

Larger mammals live in arid regions too. Fennecs, a very small fox living near sand dunes, can go a long time without drinking. Camels can use body fluids when no water is available.

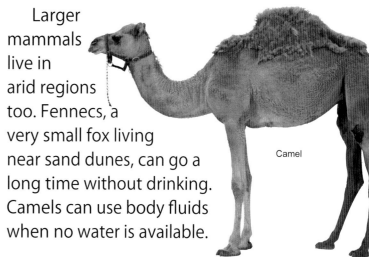
Camel

Mountain mammals

Some mammals spend most of their lives on mountain peaks. These include Asian markhor goats, American Rocky Mountain bighorn sheep and Siberian ibex. Siberian ibex can stand anyplace on any pinnacle with just enough room for its four feet. Other high mountain dwelling mammals include Snow leopards, Asian pikas and the Gunnison's prairie dog.

Snow leopard

Astonishing fact

The female lion does more than 90 per cent of the hunting while the male simply prefers to rest.

How do mammals move?

The various ways that mammals move around is diverse. They swim, run, crawl, walk, hop and some even fly.

The ways in which mammals move from place to place is greatly varied. Some mammals use four limbs to walk (such animals are referred to as quadrapedal) while others use only two (such animals are referred to as bipedal). The greatest differences in locomotion adaptation can be seen when comparing mammals from very different habitats. Dolphins, adapted for an aquatic lifestyle, have flippers to help them glide through the water. The jaguar, a terrestrial carnivore with explosive running power, is adapted for speed on land. The limbs of bats have evolved into wings enabling them to inhabit the skies.

Mammals have different ways of moving around. Bats are able to fly through the use of wings. They are the only mammals that can actually fly.

Astonishing fact

A rhinoceros' horn is made of the same material found in our hair and fingernails which is called keratin.

Flying lemurs, flying phalangers, and flying squirrels cannot actually fly. These mammals have a fold of skin between the forelimb and hindlimb on each side of the body. By stretching out these 'wings,' the animals can glide from tree to tree.

Other mammals walk using legs such as cats, dogs, horses, apes and of course, people.

Some mammals even have fins! The Fin whale is the second largest animal on earth and can reach a length of up to 27 m. The whale has a dorsal fin on the rear half of its back.

Social life

Solitary mammals

Some mammals are solitary. They keep company with another of the same kind only when mating or when raising young. Solitary mammals include the giant anteaters, European bison, and right whales.

European bison

Group living

Many mammals live in groups. In large groups, some eat, some rest, and some keep guard. Baboons, for example, may have from twenty to 300 animals in a group. One or more adult males lead each group. If a predator, such as a leopard approaches, the males take action against it, while the females and young escape.

Some mammals travel in herds. Musk oxen travel in closely packed herds of fifteen to 100 individuals. These herds include males and females. Bighorn sheep females travel in herds of five to fifteen, with a dominant ewe, or female, as the leader.

Pack mammals get their food by cooperation. They work together to bring down much larger prey. Dingoes, killer whales, and lions hunt in packs.

Astonishing fact

Giraffe's tongue's are blue and can extend more than 40 cm long.

Mammal sleeping habits

Sleep is essential for survival. Sleep deprivation is as dangerous to humans as it is to other mammals, and can lead to impaired memory, erratic behaviour and lack of coordination. Most mammals sleep, in one form or another, for at least part of their day, even if those sleep patterns differ from what we would normally consider standard sleep.

While most newborns—human and other—sleep an average of about twice as much than adults, dolphins and killer whales do not sleep at all during the first month of their lives. This gradually changes as they get older but in the first 30 days they move around in a strategy to avoid predators.

There are marked differences in the sleeping patterns of mammals according to their size and their diets. For example, herbivores sleep a lot less than carnivores and small mammals sleep more than large ones, with just a few exceptions (such as lions). This may be due to their need to stay alert to evade predators or the need to keep warm as outside temperatures drop. Animals also sleep a lot less in winter because body temperature is reduced during sleep and small mammals need to conserve as much body heat as possible to survive the outdoors.

On the other side are the mammals who spend most of their lives sleeping. Aside from hibernation, considered a form of sleep, lions and bats have the record for more hours of sleep in a single day: 19 and 17 hours respectively. The North American opossum, the owl monkey, the tiger and the squirrel all sleep more than 15 hours per day, despite season or age.

What do mammals eat?

Mammals eat many kinds of foods—plants, meat, fish, insects. Their teeth are designed for what they eat. Sharp pointed teeth are best for tearing flesh, while broad flat teeth are good for grinding up plants.

Insect-eaters

Different mammals have different feeding habits. Some are insect eating animals known as insectivores who forage for slugs, worms, insects and snails. There are around 345 mammal species that are insectivores. Most have long snouts, small eyes and very sharp teeth. Insect-eating mammals include the moles, aye-ayes and aardvarks. The aardvark has a sticky tongue that can reach out as long as 1 ft (0.3 m) to capture its ant and termite meals.

Astonishing fact

Bats live 20-30 years, which is remarkably long for such a small animal.

Plant eaters

Some mammals eat nothing but plants. Plant eaters include pandas, the West Indian manatee, and the red-bellied wallaby. Some mammals eat both plants and fruit. These include the Eurasian harvest mouse, South American capybara, and the African elephant. An elephant can eat up to 227 kg of grass, plants, and fruit per day.

South American capybara

Aardvarks

Meat eaters

Mammals eating mostly meat or fish are carnivorous. Carnivorous mammals have long, pointed, and very strong incisor teeth. Carnivores include polar bears, hyenas, walruses, etc. Many meat eaters, such as lions and wolves, are fast-moving predators that can run down prey. Their long sharp canine teeth are designed for grabbing onto and stabbing other animals. Killer Whales (or Orcas) behave much like land carnivores, chasing and killing seals, fish, and penguins. The Walrus, a carnivore, rakes the ocean floor with its long tusks, looking for clams to eat.

Omnivores

Omnivores are mammals that eat both plants and animals as their primary food source. Pigs are one well-known example of an omnivore. Humans are also omnivores. Most bear species are considered omnivores, however, individuals diets can range from almost exclusively herbivorous to almost exclusively carnivorous depending on what food sources are available in their environments and what season of the year it is.

Microscopic diet

The largest mammals in the world eat the smallest foods. Blue and Humpback Whales feed on tiny plants called plankton. Instead of teeth, their mouths have large brush like structures called baleen. As water rushes into a whale's mouth, the baleen strains out the plankton.

Walrus

Humpback Whales

Adaptations

Species of mammals have developed a variety of adaptations in response to the different environments in which they live. Mammals in cold climates have insulating layers consisting of a thick coat of fur or a thick layer of fat (blubber). This layer helps retain body heat and keeps the animal's body temperature constant. Some mammals that live in deserts survive by special adaptations in their kidneys and sweat glands that allow them to survive when only very small amounts of water are available to them. The kangaroo rats of the deserts of the south-western United States are known for their ability to live on a diet of dry seeds and no drinking water.

Some small mammals can avoid the intense cold and food shortages of winter by hibernating. Some species of ground squirrel store much of the energy derived from feeding in the summer as fat, which

Astonishing fact

The northern hairy-nosed wombat is one of the world's rarest mammals.

provides the energy that sustains the squirrels during six months of winter dormancy. Conversely, a similar adaptation to the harshness of some summer habitats is aestivation, or summer dormancy. Some animals both hibernate and aestivate and are active only during the relatively mild seasons in between.

Mammals are the only animals that have hair covering their body, a rod of cells that are strengthened by the protein keratin. The different types of hair mammals have include fur, whiskers, spines, and horns. Fur provides protection for the skin and insulates the animal. Whiskers provide sensory information for animals. Spines (such as the quills of a porcupine) provide protection.

Arctic fox

Means of defence

For a wild animal, surviving each day can be hard. Carnivores use speed, strength, and intelligence to catch a meal. Prey species often have to think fast to protect themselves.

Some methods include disguises and deceit to fool its enemy into retreat. One method used in this type of defence is camouflage. Some animals can change their own colouring to match their surroundings. Others are born with the colouring that will allow them to blend into their native surroundings. The white coat of the arctic fox and the polar bear provide excellent cover against the white snow of its homeland.

A more direct line of defence would be actual weapons, evolved over thousands of years that best defend each animal. One is the antler, tusk or horn. Antlers, mostly found in the deer family, which includes elk, caribou and moose, are used to charge and duel with an enemy. Another weapon found in the animal world are claws. Many animals have claws that are so sharp they will cut through flesh on the first swipe. A few of these animals are the bear and all members of the cat family. A few animals have the ability to ward off predators at long range. One such animal is the skunk. Known for its bad odour, the skunk can drive away enemies by using its powerful scent glands. Other animals that use this method are weasels, foxes, mink and wolverines.

Many of the features common to most animals can be used in defence, including the feet, tongue and tail. Many animals have developed large powerful feet which they use to kick or stomp on their enemies, such as the rabbit, elephant and kangaroo.

Skunk

Astonishing fact

Camels have a split upper lip, which aids them in grazing.

Significance

About 14,000 years ago, humans began controlling or domesticating certain animals. This made human lives easier. Horses have been domesticated for practical uses, such as transportation and for entertainment such as horse riding and racing.

People use mammals for many purposes. Cows provide meat, milk, cheese, butter and hide. Camels, yaks, and Indian elephants carry or pull heavy items. Water buffaloes do hauling and can provide milk. Horses provide transportation and racing activities. Other domesticated animals include rabbits, pigs, goats, sheep, cavies and capybaras.

People keep animals as pets. Common mammal pets are dogs, cats, guinea pigs, and hamsters.

Of about 5,000 mammal species currently existing, over 1,000 are seriously endangered. Few wild mammals can live

Astonishing fact

Flippers of the humpback whale can grow as long as 15 ft.

outside their natural habitat. When land is cleared for farming or housing, animals making homes there must leave, if there is any place for them to go. If not, they die from starvation or from predators.

Many human habits have also led to endangerment. Hunting for amusement, killing for fur or body parts, native and commercial killing for food, illegal pet trade and chemicals have all taken their toll.

Some mammals are probably on the way to extinction, or total elimination. There are only about sixty Javan rhinoceros left in the world. The Seychelles sheath-tailed bat has only about fifty individuals remaining. Yellow-tailed woolly monkeys number no more than 250 individuals. Mediterranean monk seals number only 600 individuals.

Seychelles sheath-tailed bat

Today many people are trying to save endangered animals. Methods include zoo breeding, establishing forest reserves, and training native populations that animals can be an economic benefit. There are laws against importing and exporting endangered species. And, in some parts of the world, there are laws against land destruction.

Some mammals have possibly been rescued from immediate extinction. The American bison once roamed the North American prairies, numbering about 50 million. After slaughter by soldiers and settlers for food and sport, by 1889 only 541 remained alive. Now, in the United States, there are about 35,000 in protected areas. The Mongolian wild horse, once thought to be extinct, now has a special reserve in Mongolia.

Some mammals became extinct only

Astonishing fact

Giant flying foxes (fruit bats) that live in Indonesia have wingspans of nearly five feet.

recently. Recently extinct animals include Steller's sea cows, which became extinct in about 1768. The Tasmanian wolf was last seen in 1933, eliminated by hunters. The African blue buck disappeared from Earth in 1880. The Quagga, from southern Asia, was hunted for hides and meat. The last known Quagga, a relative of the zebra, died in a Dutch zoo in 1883.

Javan rhinoceros

Mammal extremes

Fastest mammal (also the fastest land animal)	The Cheetah (97-110 kph)
Slowest mammal	The Sloth (2 kph)
Biggest mammal, biggest animal that ever lived on Earth	The Blue Whale
Biggest land mammal	The African Elephant
Tallest mammal	The Giraffe
Smallest mammals	A bat from Thailand, Kitli's Hog-nosed Bat, being only 1.14-1.3 inches long and weighing a mere 1.7-2 g
Loudest mammal	The Blue Whale. The second loudest is the Howler Monkey
Smelliest mammal	The Striped Skunk
The only venomous mammals	Duckbilled platypus (males only), several species of shrews, and the Solenodon
Fat	The Blue Whale has the thickest layer of blubber, but Ringed Seal pups have the greatest percentage of fat (about 50 per cent).
Longest lived mammals	Whales

Some well-known mammals

Blue Whale

By considerable measure, the largest known animal on Earth is the blue whale. Mature blue whales can measure anywhere from 23 m to 30.5 m from head to tail, and can weigh as much as 150 tons. That's as long as an 8 to 10 storey building and as heavy as about 112 adult male giraffes! Female blue whales generally weigh more than the males. It is also the loudest animal on Earth.

A blue whale's heart is as big as a small car, and its arteries are wide enough that you could climb through them. Even baby blue whales dwarf most animals. At birth, a blue whale calf is about 7.6 m long and weighs more than an elephant. And they grow up fast. During the first 7 months of its life, a blue whale drinks approximately 379 l of its mother's milk per day, putting on as much as 91 kg every 24 hours. It takes about 3600 kg of fresh seafood a day to keep the blue whale well fed.

Blue whales live at the surface of the ocean and are found in all the oceans of the world.

Pangolin

Although it looks like a scaly reptile, the pangolin is indeed a mammal. There are eight different species of pangolins found in the tropical regions of Africa and Asia. The most common species of pangolin are the giant pangolin (most threatened), the tree pangolin and the most widespread, the ground pangolin.

Pangolins are toothless and have no external ears, though their hearing is reportedly very good. Since they have no teeth, they have a gizzard like stomach and swallow small stones and sand to help with the digestive process. Pangolins have very long tongues up to 16 inches in length which they use to gulp up termites and ants.

They have a good sense of smell and a poor sense of sight. Their scales, made out of keratin (same material that makes up human fingernails), make up 20 per cent of their total body weight. These scales are used for defence. If threatened, the pangolin will roll itself up into a tight ball which is very difficult to unroll. The scales are razor sharp and combined with powerful muscles can inflict serious wounds. As a last defensive resort, pangolins also have anal scent glands that emit strong, foul smelling secretions.

Pangolins are nocturnal. Tree dwelling pangolins live in hollow trees, whereas the ground dwelling species dig tunnels underground, up to a depth of 3.5 m. They are also very good swimmers.

Echidna

Together with the platypus, echidnas are the world's only monotremes, or egg-laying mammals. There are two species of echidnas, one confined to the highlands of New Guinea, and one which lives in Australia and New Guinea. All echidnas have sharp spines covering the back of their short, stocky bodies.

The echidna's snout is between 7 and 8 cm long, and is stiffened to enable the animal to break up logs and termite mounds when searching for food. Adult echidnas vary in size, from 35 to 53 cm. Males weigh about 6 kg, while females weigh about 4.5 kg.

The short, stout limbs of an echidna are well-suited for scratching and digging in the soil. The front feet have five flattened claws which are used to dig forest litter, burrow, and tear open logs and termite mounds. The hind feet point backwards, and help to push soil away when the animal is burrowing. Two of the claws on each back foot are used for grooming. An echidna's tail is short, stubby and hairless underneath.

The echidna looks fearsome enough,

but it is a shy animal and would rather retreat than fight if disturbed. When frightened, it will curl into a ball, with its snout and legs tucked beneath it, and its sharp spines sticking out. It will wedge itself beneath rocks, or burrow straight down into soft soil, to escape predators such as dogs, eagles and dingoes.

With a keen sense of smell, an echidna uses its long, hairless snout to search for

food, detect danger and locate other echidnas. Termites are the preferred food, which is why the animal is often called the 'spiny anteater'. After finding food, an echidna catches the prey with its long, sticky tongue. As it has no teeth, it grinds its food between its tongue and the bottom of its mouth.

Dugong

Dugong

The dugong is a large marine mammal found in the warm waters surrounding Indonesia and Australia. Dugongs are around 3 m and weigh nearly 400 kg.

It is thought the legends of mermaids may have originated when sailors from a distance glimpsed dugongs swimming in the water, and mistook them for half-human half-fish creatures.

Dugongs inhabit the warm shallow waters, and despite their large size, dugongs are strictly herbivorous animals and have been referred to as the cows of the sea. Dugongs graze on sea grasses and aquatic plants that grow in abundance in the tropical shallows. Dugongs eat large amounts of sea plants and often leave feeding trails behind of bare sand and uprooted sea grass. They are long-lived as well and can live up to 70 years

Duck-Billed Platypus

Duckbill Platypus or Duck Mole is an egg-laying mammal of Australia. Platypuses and echidnas, collectively called monotremes, are unique among mammals in that they lay eggs.

The platypus's body is about 20 inches (50 cm) long and covered with greyish-brown fur. The tail is broad and short. The platypus has acute vision and hearing. Its ears are located in furrows behind the eyes. The animal's jaws extend in a duck-like bill covered with smooth, black, sensitive, leathery skin. The feet are webbed and the membranes of the front feet fold back into the palms to expose sharp digging claws. For defence, it is venomous. The male platypus has a spur on the hind foot that delivers a venom capable of causing severe, unbearable (though not lethal) pain to humans

Puma

The Puma is also known as the Mountain Lion, Cougar or Panther. It is one of the largest and ruthless members of the cat family in the world.

The puma is brown or tan in colour with short to medium-length fur, depending on the climate in which it lives.

The Puma is a carnivorous stalker and ambush predator and pursues a wide variety of prey. Their main diet consists of deer, horses, elk, cattle and sheep. Basically, the puma will eat any animal it can catch, even animals as large as a moose. Pumas will stalk their prey through bushes and trees and across rock ledges before powerfully leaping onto the back of their victim and delivering a suffocating neck bite.

Cheetah

The cheetah is the world's fastest land mammal. While running, they cover 6 to 6.7 m in one stride, about the same distance as a racehorse. Cheetahs are off the ground more than half of their running time! Their claws are hard and sharp, giving them great footing when they run.

Chasing prey is hard on a cheetah. Once caught, a cheetah holds its prey with a strangling bite to the neck. The cheetah is panting intensely, and its body temperature can reach as high as 41 degrees Celsius. It takes 20 minutes for its breathing and temperature to return to normal, the same time it takes for the prey to suffocate.

Once they have recovered, cheetahs must eat quickly, as they can be driven off by leopards, lions or hyenas. Cheetahs aren't strong enough to hide or guard their catch, so they have only one chance to eat their meal.

Puma

Bactrian Camel

An imposing animal, the Bactrian camel can reach 7 ft in height and weigh up to 681.82kg. The species thick, brown coat changes with the seasons. During winter, it thickens to provide added insulation against the cold while large chunks of fur are shed in the summer to keep the animal cool. Both male and female Bactrian camels have two large humps on their backs.

This camel is probably the ancestor of all domestic two-humped camels. The species can withstand drought, food shortages and even radiation from nuclear weapons testing. Fewer than 1,000 individuals survive today in only four locations. Classified as Critically Endangered, these animals continue to be threatened by hunting, habitat loss, and competition for resources with introduced livestock.

The species has suffered a drastic reduction in its range. It now occurs only in three separated habitats in northwest China (Lake Lob, Taklimakan desert and the ranges of Arjin Shan) and one in the Trans-Altai Gobi desert of southwest Mongolia. The largest population lives in the Gashun Gobi (Lop Nur) Desert in Xinjiang Province, China, which was for 45 years used as a test site for nuclear weapons.

Bactrians rarely sweat, helping them conserve fluids for long periods of time. In winter, plants may yield enough moisture to sustain a camel without water for several weeks.

When camels do refill, however, they soak up water like a sponge. A very thirsty animal can drink 135 litres of water in only 13 minutes.

African elephant

African Elephant

The African elephant is the largest living land mammal. These mammals have very strong social bonds and live in family groups headed by a female (called a cow). Males (called bulls) occasionally join the group. Elephants are excellent swimmers. Elephants have few natural enemies except man, and they are in danger of extinction due to loss of habitat and poaching for their ivory tusks. African elephants average about 3 m tall at the shoulder, weighing roughly 5,400 kg. Males are larger than females. Both males and females have tusks (large, pointed ivory teeth). They have wrinkled, gray-brown skin that is almost hairless. Elephants eat roots, grasses, leaves, fruit, and bark. They use their tusks and trunk to get food. These herbivores spend most of their time eating. Bulls can eat up to 130-260 kg of food each day.

Aardvark

Aardvark is an African mammal. The name means 'earth pig' in Afrikaans and refers to its resemblance to a pig and to its habit of digging. The aardvark is 1.4 to 2.1 m long, including the muscular, 2 ft (60 cm) tail. It weighs 50 to 70 kg. The aardvark has a long, narrow head, long ears, and a blunt snout. It has teeth that grow continuously throughout its life. The aardvark forages for termites and ants in the late afternoon and evening over a large home range. Since it has poor eyesight, it swings its nose through the air from side to side to pick up the scent of food. When it locates a large termite mound or ant hill, it digs into it with its powerful front legs, keeping its ears upright to listen for predators. It can take up to 50,000 insects in one night with its super sticky tongue.

Giraffe

The giraffe is the tallest living animal which is instantly recognizable by its exceptionally long neck. Adult males stand 4.6 - 6.0 m tall, whereas females are shorter at 4 - 4.8 m tall. In addition to its great height, the giraffe is also one of the heaviest land animals. Exceptionally large males may weigh up to 1,900 kg.

Giraffes are plant-eaters, eating mostly leaves, twigs and bark from the tops of the thorny acacia plant. The giraffes carefully eat around the thorns, and their tough lips and thick saliva protect them from the thorns.

Acacia leaves contain a lot of water, so giraffes can go a long time without drinking. When they do get thirsty, giraffes have to bend a long way down to drink from a lake or stream. When they are bent over, it is easier for a predator, like a crocodile, to grab hold of the giraffe. So, giraffes go to a watering hole together and take turns watching for predators. If water is easily available, they can drink 10 gallons or 38 litres a day.

All mammals have fur or hair on their bodies. Giraffes are no exception. But a giraffe's coat is special because it is like a fingerprint. Each giraffe has its own distinct pattern. Even within the same group of giraffes, no two coats are identical. A baby giraffe can recognize its mother by her unique coat pattern.

The giraffe has keen sight and hearing. It can run up to 47 km/h and can usually outrun predators. Giraffes have been known to kill lions, their principal enemies, by kicking with their powerful legs. Giraffes were formerly killed by hunters for their hide and meat. They are now protected by law and most are found in game preserves.

27

Red Kangaroo

The red kangaroo is the world's biggest marsupial. An average-sized red kangaroo stands about 1.5 m tall and can weigh 85 kg. Female red kangaroos are smaller, lighter, and faster than males. They also have a blue-hued coat; so many Australians call them 'blue fliers'.

Red kangaroos hop along on their powerful hind legs and do so at great speed. A red kangaroo can reach speeds of over 56 km an hour. Their bounding gate allows them to cover 8 m in a single leap and to jump 1.8 m high.

The Red Kangaroo is found in a variety of habitats throughout Australia and New Zealand.

Tasmanian Devil

The Tasmanian devil cannot be mistaken for any other marsupial. Its spine-chilling screeches, black colour, and reputed bad-temper, led the early European settlers to call it The Devil. Although only the size of a small dog, it can sound and look incredibly fierce.

The Tasmanian devil is the world's largest carnivorous marsupial, reaching 30 inches in length and weighing up to 12 kg. Its oversized head houses sharp teeth and strong, muscular jaws that can deliver one of the most powerful bites of any mammal.

Though once found throughout Australia, Tasmanian devils now only inhabit the island of Tasmania. Tasmanian devils store fat in their tails, so a fatter tail means a healthier devil. Today, a disease threatens these rare and unique marsupials and could ultimately lead to their extinction.

Red kangaroo

Tasmanian devil

Orangutan

The Malay word orangutan means 'person of the forest.' These long-haired primates, found only in Sumatra and Borneo, are highly intelligent and are close relatives of humans.

Orangutans have distinctive body shapes with very long arms that may reach up to two metres in length. They have a coarse, shaggy reddish coat and grasping hands and feet. Orangutans spend most of their lives in trees. They use their long, powerful arms to swing from one branch to another. Their thumbs and big toes allow them to grasp things with their hands and feet. Orangutans feed mainly on fruit, insects, and leaves. At night they gather leaves and twigs and build a large platform-like nest on which they sleep. Orangutans typically live alone or in small groups. Their average life span is 30 years.

Due to commercial logging and illegal hunting, the orangutan is an endangered species.

Slender Loris

The Slender loris is a small tree dwelling mammal. They are found only in the tropical rainforests of Southern India and Sri Lanka.

The Slender Loris has the unique ability to stretch and twist their long arms and legs through the branches of the trees without alerting their prey, to capture their favourite foods - poisonous and bad smelling insects. They particularly like the acacia ant whose bite can numb a human arm. They also like toxic beetles and roaches. To defend against the sting of some of these toxic insects, they engage in urine washing during which they rub urine all over their hands, feet and face which soothes the sting.

Orangutan

Slender loris

Polar Bear

Polar bears are large, meat-eating bears who are well-adapted for life in their frozen Arctic environment. They are powerful swimmers who hunt seals in the water. Polar bears can run in bursts up to 40 kph.

Polar bears are up to 3 m long and weigh about 770 kg. Polar bears have a small head, powerful jaws, and a black nose and tongue. They have a strong sense of smell. They have wide front paws with slightly webbed toes that help them swim. These bears paddle with their front feet and steer with the hind feet. Polar bears have two types of fur. They have thick, woolly fur close to the skin that keeps them warm. They also have hollow guard hairs that stick up and protect the bears from getting wet. These guard hairs are like drinking straws and are clear-coloured (not white). The white-looking coat camouflages them well in the snow and ice. Under the fur, Polar bears have black skin. They also have a thick layer of fat (up to 4 inches thick) under the skin that helps keep them warm.

Polar bears live in icy Arctic areas of Alaska, Canada, Greenland, Norway, and Russia. They spend much of their time swimming in frigid seas.

Polar bears are mainly meat eaters, and their favourite food is seal. They will also eat walrus, caribou, beached whales, grass, and seaweed. Polar bears are patient hunters, staying motionless for hours above a seal's breathing hole in the ice, just waiting for a seal to pop up. Polar bears don't drink water.

The polar bear's nose is so powerful it can smell a seal on the ice 32 km away, sniff out a seal's den that has been covered with snow, and even find a seal's air hole in the ice up to 1.6 km away. No wonder many people call them 'noses with legs!'

Test Your MEMORY

1. When did mammals evolve?

2. How many species of mammals are there in the world today?

3. Name the three types of mammals.

4. Name the two monotremes.

5. Write any two characteristics of mammals.

6. Name two mountain mammals.

7. What do mammals eat?

8. Name the fastest dog on earth.

9. Write about the means of defence used by the Skunk.

10. Name the biggest mammal in the world.

11. What are the other names for the Puma?

12. Name the fastest land mammal in the world.

Index